INTRODUCTION

The Lord Jesus, on the night before he suffered on the cross, shared one last meal with his disciples. During this meal our Savior instituted the sacrament of his Body and Blood. He did this in order to perpetuate the sacrifice of the Cross throughout the ages and to entrust to the Church his Spouse a memorial of his death and resurrection. As the Gospel of Matthew tells us:

> While they were eating, Jesus took bread, said the blessing, broke it, and giving it to his disciples said, "Take and eat; this is my body." Then he took a cup, gave thanks, and gave it to them, saying, "Drink from it, all of you, for this is my blood of the covenant, which will be shed on behalf of many for the forgiveness of sins." (Mt 26:26-28; cf. Mk 14:22-24, Lk 22:17-20, 1 Cor 11:23-25)

Recalling these words of Jesus, the Catholic Church professes that, in the celebration of the Eucharist, bread and wine become the Body and Blood of Jesus Christ through the power of the Holy Spirit and the instrumentality of the priest. Jesus said: "I am the living bread that came down from heaven; whoever eats this bread will live forever; and the bread that I will give is my flesh for the life of the world. . . . For my flesh is true food, and my blood is true drink" (Jn 6:51-55). The whole Christ is truly present, body, blood, soul, and divinity, under the appearances of bread and wine—the glorified Christ who rose from the dead after dying for our sins. This is what the Church means when she speaks of the "Real Presence" of Christ in the Eucharist. This presence of Christ in the

Eucharist is called "real" not to exclude other types of his presence as if they could not be understood as real (cf. *Catechism*, no. 1374). The risen Christ is present to his Church in many ways, but most especially through the sacrament of his Body and Blood.

What does it mean that Jesus Christ is present in the Eucharist under the appearances of bread and wine? How does this happen? The presence of the risen Christ in the Eucharist is an inexhaustible mystery that the Church can never fully explain in words. We must remember that the triune God is the creator of all that exists and has the power to do more than we can possibly imagine. As St. Ambrose said: "If the word of the Lord Jesus is so powerful as to bring into existence things which were not, then *a fortiori* those things which already exist can be changed into something else" (*De Sacramentis*, IV, 5-16). God created the world in order to share his life with persons who are not God. This great plan of salvation reveals a wisdom that surpasses our understanding. But we are not left in ignorance: for out of his love for us, God reveals his truth to us in ways that we can understand through the gift of faith and the grace of the Holy Spirit dwelling in us. We are thus enabled to understand at least in some measure what would otherwise remain unknown to us, though we can never completely comprehend the mystery of God.

As successors of the Apostles and teachers of the Church, the bishops have the duty to hand on what God has revealed to us and to encourage all members of the Church to deepen their understanding of the mystery and gift of the Eucharist. In order to foster such a deepening of faith, we have prepared this text to respond to fifteen questions that commonly arise with regard to the Real Presence of Christ in the Eucharist. We offer this text to pastors and religious educators to assist them in their teaching responsibilities. We recognize that some of these questions involve rather complex theological ideas. It is our hope, however, that study and discussion of the text will aid many of the Catholic faithful in our country to enrich their understanding of this mystery of the faith.

1 WHY DOES JESUS GIVE HIMSELF TO US AS FOOD AND DRINK?

Jesus gives himself to us in the Eucharist as spiritual nourishment because he loves us. God's whole plan for our salvation is directed to our participation in the life of the Trinity, the communion of Father, Son, and Holy Spirit. Our sharing in this life begins with our Baptism, when by the power of the Holy Spirit we are joined to Christ, thus becoming adopted sons and daughters of the Father. It is strengthened and increased in Confirmation. It is nourished and deepened through our participation in the Eucharist. By eating the Body and drinking the Blood of Christ in the Eucharist we become united to the person of Christ through his humanity. "Whoever eats my flesh and drinks my blood remains in me and I in him" (Jn 6:56). In being united to the humanity of Christ we are at the same time united to his divinity. Our mortal and corruptible natures are transformed by being joined to the source of life. "Just as the living Father sent me and I have life because of the Father, so also the one who feeds on me will have life because of me" (Jn 6:57).

By being united to Christ through the power of the Holy Spirit dwelling in us, we are drawn up into the eternal relationship of love among the

Father, the Son, and the Holy Spirit. As Jesus is the eternal Son of God by nature, so we become sons and daughters of God by adoption through the sacrament of Baptism. Through the sacraments of Baptism and Confirmation (Chrismation), we are temples of the Holy Spirit, who dwells in us, and by his indwelling we are made holy by the gift of sanctifying grace. The ultimate promise of the Gospel is that we will share in the life of the Holy Trinity. The Fathers of the Church called this participation in the divine life "divinization" (*theosis*). In this we see that God does not merely send us good things from on high; instead, we are brought up into the inner life of God, the communion among the Father, the Son, and the Holy Spirit. In the celebration of the Eucharist (which means "thanksgiving") we give praise and glory to God for this sublime gift.

2 WHY IS THE EUCHARIST NOT ONLY A MEAL BUT ALSO A SACRIFICE?

While our sins would have made it impossible for us to share in the life of God, Jesus Christ was sent to remove this obstacle. His death was a sacrifice for our sins. Christ is "the Lamb of God, who takes away the sin of the world" (Jn 1:29). Through his death and resurrection, he conquered sin and death and reconciled us to God. The Eucharist is the memorial of this sacrifice. The Church gathers to remember and to re-present the sacrifice of Christ in which we share through the action of the priest and the power of the Holy Spirit. Through the celebration of the Eucharist, we are joined to Christ's sacrifice and receive its inexhaustible benefits.

As the Letter to the Hebrews explains, Jesus is the one eternal high priest who always lives to make intercession for the people before the

Father. In this way, he surpasses the many high priests who over centuries used to offer sacrifices for sin in the Jerusalem temple. The eternal high priest Jesus offers the perfect sacrifice which is his very self, not something else. "He entered once for all into the sanctuary, not with the blood of goats and calves but with his own blood, thus obtaining eternal redemption" (Heb 9:12).

Jesus' act belongs to human history, for he is truly human and has entered into history. At the same time, however, Jesus Christ is the Second Person of the Holy Trinity; he is the eternal Son, who is not confined within time or history. His actions transcend time, which is part of creation. "Passing through the greater and more perfect tabernacle not made by hands, that is, not belonging to this creation" (Heb 9:11), Jesus the eternal Son of God made his act of sacrifice in the presence of his Father, who lives in eternity. Jesus' one perfect sacrifice is thus eternally present before the Father, who eternally accepts it. This means that in the Eucharist, Jesus does not sacrifice himself again and again. Rather, by the power of the Holy Spirit his one eternal sacrifice is made present once again, re-presented, so that we may share in it.

Christ does not have to leave where he is in heaven to be with us. Rather, we partake of the heavenly liturgy where Christ eternally intercedes for us and presents his sacrifice to the Father and where the angels and saints constantly glorify God and give thanks for all his gifts: "To the one who sits on the throne and to the Lamb be blessing and honor, glory and might, forever and ever" (Rev 5:13). As the *Catechism of the Catholic Church* states, "By the Eucharistic celebration we already unite

ourselves with the heavenly liturgy and antici-
pate eternal life, when God will be all in all" (no.
1326). The *Sanctus* proclamation, "Holy, Holy,
Holy Lord . . . ," is the song of the angels who
are in the presence of God (Is 6:3). When in the
Eucharist we proclaim the *Sanctus* we echo on
earth the song of angels as they worship God in
heaven. In the eucharistic celebration we do not
simply remember an event in history. Rather,
through the mysterious action of the Holy Spirit
in the eucharistic celebration the Lord's Paschal
Mystery is made present and contemporaneous
to his Spouse the Church.

Furthermore, in the eucharistic re-presentation
of Christ's eternal sacrifice before the Father, we
are not simply spectators. The priest and the
worshiping community are in different ways
active in the eucharistic sacrifice. The ordained
priest standing at the altar represents Christ as
head of the Church. All the baptized, as members of Christ's Body, share in his priesthood, as
both priest and victim. The Eucharist is also the
sacrifice of the Church. The Church, which is
the Body and Bride of Christ, participates in the
sacrificial offering of her Head and Spouse. In
the Eucharist, the sacrifice of Christ becomes
the sacrifice of the members of his Body who
united to Christ form one sacrificial offering
(cf. *Catechism*, no. 1368). As Christ's sacrifice is
made sacramentally present, united with Christ,
we offer ourselves as a sacrifice to the Father.
"The whole Church exercises the role of priest
and victim along with Christ, offering the
Sacrifice of the Mass and itself completely
offered in it" (*Mysterium Fidei*, no. 31; cf.
Lumen Gentium, no. 11).

3 WHEN THE BREAD AND WINE BECOME THE BODY AND BLOOD OF CHRIST, WHY DO THEY STILL LOOK AND TASTE LIKE BREAD AND WINE?

In the celebration of the Eucharist, the glorified Christ becomes present under the appearances of bread and wine in a way that is unique, a way that is uniquely suited to the Eucharist. In the Church's traditional theological language, in the act of consecration during the Eucharist the "substance" of the bread and wine is changed by the power of the Holy Spirit into the "substance" of the Body and Blood of Jesus Christ. At the same time, the "accidents" or appearances of bread and wine remain. "Substance" and "accident" are here used as philosophical terms that have been adapted by great medieval theologians such as St. Thomas Aquinas in their efforts to understand and explain the faith. Such terms are used to convey the fact that what appears to be bread and wine in every way (at the level of "accidents" or physical attributes—that is, what can be seen, touched, tasted, or measured) in fact is now the Body and Blood of Christ (at the level of "substance" or deepest reality). This change at the level of substance from bread and wine into the Body and Blood of Christ is called "transubstantiation." According to Catholic faith, we can speak of the Real Presence of Christ in the Eucharist because this transubstantiation has occurred (cf. *Catechism*, no. 1376).

This is a great mystery of our faith—we can only know it from Christ's teaching given us in the Scriptures and in the Tradition of the Church. Every other change that occurs in the world involves a change in accidents or characteristics. Sometimes the accidents change while the substance remains the same. For example, when a child reaches adulthood, the characteristics of the human person change in many ways, but the adult remains the same person—the same substance. At other times, the substance and the accidents both change. For example, when a person eats an apple, the apple is incorporated into the body of that person—is changed into the body of that person. When this change of substance occurs, however, the accidents or characteristics of the apple do not remain. As the apple is changed into the body of the person, it takes on the accidents or characteristics of the body of that person. Christ's presence in the Eucharist is unique in that, even though the consecrated bread and wine truly are in substance the Body and Blood of Christ, they have none of the accidents or characteristics of a human body, but only those of bread and wine.

4 DOES THE BREAD CEASE TO BE BREAD AND THE WINE CEASE TO BE WINE?

Yes. In order for the whole Christ to be present—body, blood, soul, and divinity—the bread and wine cannot remain, but must give way so that his glorified Body and Blood may be present. Thus in the Eucharist the bread ceases to be bread in substance, and becomes the Body of Christ, while the wine ceases to be wine in substance, and becomes the Blood of Christ. As St. Thomas Aquinas observed, Christ is not quoted as saying, "*This bread* is my body," but "*This* is my body" (*Summa Theologiae*, III q. 78, a. 5).

5 IS IT FITTING THAT CHRIST'S BODY AND BLOOD BECOME PRESENT IN THE EUCHARIST UNDER THE APPEARANCES OF BREAD AND WINE?

Yes, for this way of being present corresponds perfectly to the sacramental celebration of the

Eucharist. Jesus Christ gives himself to us in a form that employs the symbolism inherent in eating bread and drinking wine. Furthermore, being present under the appearances of bread and wine, Christ gives himself to us in a form that is appropriate for human eating and drinking. Also, this kind of presence corresponds to the virtue of faith, for the presence of the Body and Blood of Christ cannot be detected or discerned by any way other than faith. That is why St. Bonaventure affirmed: "There is no difficulty over Christ's being present in the sacrament as in a sign; the great difficulty is in the fact that He is really in the sacrament, as He is in heaven. And so believing this is especially meritorious" (*In IV Sent.*, dist. X, P. I, art. un., qu. I). On the authority of God who reveals himself to us, by faith we believe that which cannot be grasped by our human faculties (cf. *Catechism*, no. 1381).

6 ARE THE CONSECRATED BREAD AND WINE "MERELY SYMBOLS"?

In everyday language, we call a "symbol" something that points beyond itself to something else, often to several other realities at once. The transformed bread and wine that are the Body and Blood of Christ are not merely symbols because they truly are the Body and Blood of Christ. As St. John Damascene wrote: "The bread and wine are not a foreshadowing of the body and blood of Christ—By no means!—but the actual deified body of the Lord, because the Lord Himself said: 'This is my body'; not 'a foreshadowing of my body' but 'my body,' and not 'a foreshadowing of my blood' but 'my blood'" (*The Orthodox Faith*, IV [PG 94, 1148-49]).

At the same time, however, it is important to recognize that the Body and Blood of Christ come to us in the Eucharist in a sacramental form. In other words, Christ is present under the appearances of bread and wine, not in his own proper form. We cannot presume to know all the reasons behind God's actions. God uses, however, the symbolism inherent in the eating of bread and the drinking of wine at the natural level to illuminate the meaning of what is being accomplished in the Eucharist through Jesus Christ.

There are various ways in which the symbolism of eating bread and drinking wine discloses the meaning of the Eucharist. For example, just as natural food gives nourishment to the body, so the eucharistic food gives spiritual nourishment. Furthermore, the sharing of an ordinary meal establishes a certain communion among the people who share it; in the Eucharist, the People of God share a meal that brings them into communion not only with each other but with the Father, Son, and Holy Spirit. Similarly, as St. Paul tells us, the single loaf that is shared among many during the eucharistic meal is an indication of the unity of those who have been called together by the Holy Spirit as one body, the Body of Christ (1 Cor 10:17). To take another example, the individual grains of wheat and individual grapes have to be harvested and to undergo a process of grinding or crushing before they are unified as bread and as wine. Because of this, bread and wine point to both the union of the many that takes place in the Body of Christ and the suffering undergone by Christ, a suffering that must also be embraced by his disciples. Much more could be said about the many ways in which the eating of bread and drinking of wine symbolize what God does for us through Christ, since symbols carry multiple meanings and connotations.

7 DO THE CONSECRATED BREAD AND WINE CEASE TO BE THE BODY AND BLOOD OF CHRIST WHEN THE MASS IS OVER?

No. During the celebration of the Eucharist, the bread and wine become the Body and Blood of Christ, and this they remain. They cannot turn back into bread and wine, for they are no longer bread and wine at all. There is thus no reason for them to change back to their "normal" state after the special circumstances of the Mass are past. Once the substance has really changed, the presence of the Body and Blood of Christ "endures as long as the Eucharistic species subsist" (*Catechism*, no. 1377). Against those who maintained that the bread that is consecrated during the Eucharist has no sanctifying power if it is left over until the next day, St. Cyril of Alexandria replied, "Christ is not altered, nor is his holy body changed, but the power of the consecration and his life-giving grace is perpetual in it" (*Letter 83, to Calosyrius, Bishop of Arsinoe* [PG 76, 1076]). The Church teaches that Christ remains present under the appearances of bread and wine as long as the appearances of bread and wine remain (cf. *Catechism*, no. 1377).

8 WHY ARE SOME OF THE CONSECRATED HOSTS RESERVED AFTER THE MASS?

While it would be possible to eat all of the bread that is consecrated during the Mass, some is usually kept in the tabernacle. The Body of Christ under the appearance of bread that is kept or "reserved" after the Mass is commonly referred to as the "Blessed Sacrament." There are several pastoral reasons for reserving the Blessed Sacrament. First of all, it is used for distribution to the dying (*Viaticum*), the sick, and those who legitimately cannot be present for the celebration of the Eucharist. Secondly, the Body of Christ in the form of bread is to be adored when it is exposed, as in the Rite of Eucharistic Exposition and Benediction, when it is carried in eucharistic processions, or when it is simply placed in the tabernacle, before which people pray privately. These devotions are based on the fact that Christ himself is present under the appearance of bread. Many holy people well known to American Catholics, such as St. John Neumann, St. Elizabeth Ann Seton, St. Katharine Drexel, and Blessed Damien of Molokai, practiced great personal devotion to Christ present in the Blessed Sacrament. In the Eastern Catholic Churches, devotion to the reserved Blessed Sacrament is practiced most directly at the Divine Liturgy of the Presanctified Gifts, offered on weekdays of Lent.

9 WHAT ARE APPROPRIATE SIGNS OF REVERENCE WITH RESPECT TO THE BODY AND BLOOD OF CHRIST?

The Body and Blood of Christ present under the appearances of bread and wine are treated with the greatest reverence both during and after the celebration of the Eucharist (cf. *Mysterium Fidei*, nos. 56-61). For example, the tabernacle in which the consecrated bread is reserved is placed "in some part of the church or oratory which is distinguished, conspicuous, beautifully decorated, and suitable for prayer" (*Code of Canon Law*, Can. 938, §2). According to the tradition of the Latin Church, one should genuflect in the presence of the tabernacle containing the reserved sacrament. In the Eastern Catholic Churches, the traditional practice is to make the sign of the cross and to bow profoundly. The liturgical gestures from both traditions reflect reverence, respect, and adoration. It is appropriate for the members of the assembly to greet each other in the gathering space of the church (that is, the vestibule or narthex), but it is not appropriate to speak in loud or boisterous tones in the body of the church (that is, the nave) because of the presence of Christ in the tabernacle. Also, the Church requires everyone to fast before receiving the Body and Blood of Christ as a sign of reverence and recollection (unless illness prevents one from doing so). In the Latin Church, one must generally fast for at least one hour; members of Eastern Catholic Churches must follow the practice established by their own Church.

10 IF SOMEONE WITHOUT FAITH EATS AND DRINKS THE CONSECRATED BREAD AND WINE, DOES HE OR SHE STILL RECEIVE THE BODY AND BLOOD OF CHRIST?

If "to receive" means "to consume," the answer is yes, for what the person consumes is the Body and Blood of Christ. If "to receive" means "to accept the Body and Blood of Christ knowingly and willingly as what they are, so as to obtain the spiritual benefit," then the answer is no. A lack of faith on the part of the person eating and drinking the Body and Blood of Christ cannot change what these are, but it does prevent the person from obtaining the spiritual benefit, which is communion with Christ. Such reception of Christ's Body and Blood would be in vain and, if done knowingly, would be sacrilegious (1 Cor 11:29). Reception of the Blessed Sacrament is not an automatic remedy. If we do not desire communion with Christ, God does not force this upon us. Rather, we must by faith accept God's offer of communion in Christ and in the Holy Spirit, and cooperate with God's grace in order to have our hearts and minds transformed and our faith and love of God increased.

11 IF A BELIEVER WHO IS CONSCIOUS OF HAVING COMMITTED A MORTAL SIN EATS AND DRINKS THE CONSECRATED BREAD AND WINE, DOES HE OR SHE STILL RECEIVE THE BODY AND BLOOD OF CHRIST?

Yes. The attitude or disposition of the recipient cannot change what the consecrated bread and wine are. The question here is thus not primarily about the nature of the Real Presence, but about how sin affects the relationship between an individual and the Lord. Before one steps forward to receive the Body and Blood of Christ in Holy Communion, one needs to be in a right relationship with the Lord and his Mystical Body, the Church—that is, in a state of grace, free of all mortal sin. While sin damages, and can even destroy, that relationship, the sacrament of Penance can restore it. St. Paul tells us that "whoever eats the bread or drinks the cup of the Lord unworthily will have to answer for the body and blood of the Lord. A person should examine himself, and so eat the bread and drink the cup" (1 Cor 11:27-28). Anyone who is conscious of having committed a mortal sin should be reconciled through the sacrament of Penance before receiving the Body and Blood of Christ, unless a grave reason exists for doing so and there is no opportunity for confession. In this case, the person is to be mindful of the obligation to make an act of perfect contrition, that is, an act of sorrow for sins that "arises from a love by which God is loved above all else" (*Catechism*, no. 1452). The act of perfect contrition must be accompanied by the firm intention of making a sacramental confession as soon as possible.

12 DOES ONE RECEIVE THE WHOLE CHRIST IF ONE RECEIVES HOLY COMMUNION UNDER A SINGLE FORM?

Yes. Christ Jesus, our Lord and Savior, is wholly present under the appearance either of bread or of wine in the Eucharist. Furthermore, Christ is wholly present in any fragment of the consecrated Host or in any drop of the Precious Blood. Nevertheless, it is especially fitting to receive Christ in both forms during the celebration of the Eucharist. This allows the Eucharist to appear more perfectly as a banquet, a banquet that is a foretaste of the banquet that will be celebrated with Christ at the end of time when the Kingdom of God is established in its fullness (cf. *Eucharisticum Mysterium*, no. 32).

13 IS CHRIST PRESENT DURING THE CELEBRATION OF THE EUCHARIST IN OTHER WAYS IN ADDITION TO HIS REAL PRESENCE IN THE BLESSED SACRAMENT?

Yes. Christ is present during the Eucharist in various ways. He is present in the person of the priest who offers the sacrifice of the Mass. According to the Constitution on the Sacred Liturgy of the Second Vatican Council, Christ is present in his Word "since it is he himself who speaks when the holy scriptures are read in the Church." He is also present in the assembled people as they pray and sing, "for he has promised 'where two or three are gathered together in my name there am I in the midst of them' (Mt 18:20)" (*Sacrosanctum Concilium*, no. 7). Furthermore, he is likewise present in other sacraments; for example, "when anybody baptizes it is really Christ himself who baptizes" (ibid.).

We speak of the presence of Christ under the appearances of bread and wine as "real" in order to emphasize the special nature of that presence. What appears to be bread and wine is in its very substance the Body and Blood of Christ. The entire Christ is present, God and man, body and blood, soul and divinity. While the other ways in which Christ is present in the celebration of the Eucharist are certainly not unreal, this way surpasses the others. "This presence is called 'real' not to exclude the idea that the others are 'real' too, but rather to indicate presence par excellence, because it is substantial and through it Christ becomes present whole and entire, God and man" (*Mysterium Fidei*, no. 39).

14 WHY DO WE SPEAK OF THE "BODY OF CHRIST" IN MORE THAN ONE SENSE?

First, the Body of Christ refers to the human body of Jesus Christ, who is the divine Word become man. During the Eucharist, the bread and wine become the Body and Blood of Christ. As human, Jesus Christ has a human body, a resurrected and glorified body that in the Eucharist is offered to us in the form of bread and wine.

Secondly, as St. Paul taught us in his letters, using the analogy of the human body, the Church is the Body of Christ, in which many members are united with Christ their head (1 Cor 10:16-17, 12:12-31; Rom 12:4-8). This reality is frequently referred to as the Mystical Body of Christ. All those united to Christ, the living and the dead, are joined together as one Body in Christ. This union is not one that can be seen by human eyes, for it is a mystical union brought about by the power of the Holy Spirit.

The Mystical Body of Christ and the eucharistic Body of Christ are inseparably linked. By Baptism we enter the Mystical Body of Christ, the Church, and by receiving the eucharistic Body of Christ we are strengthened and built up into the Mystical Body of Christ. The central act of the Church is the celebration of the Eucharist; the individual believers are sustained as members of the Church, members of the Mystical Body of Christ, through their reception of the Body of Christ in the Eucharist. Playing on the two meanings of "Body of Christ," St. Augustine tells those who are to receive the Body of Christ in the Eucharist: "Be what you see, and receive what you are" (Sermon 272). In another sermon he says, "If you receive worthily, you are what you have received" (Sermon 227).

The work of the Holy Spirit in the celebration of the Eucharist is twofold in a way that corresponds to the twofold meaning of "Body of Christ." On the one hand, it is through the power of the Holy Spirit that the risen Christ and his act of sacrifice become present. In the eucharistic prayer, the priest asks the Father to send the Holy Spirit down upon the gifts of bread and wine to transform them into the Body and Blood of Christ (a prayer known as the *epiclesis*, or "invocation upon"). On the other hand, at the same time the priest also asks the Father to send the Holy Spirit down upon the whole assembly so that "those who take part in the Eucharist may be one body and one spirit" (*Catechism*, no. 1353). It is through the Holy Spirit that the gift of the eucharistic Body of Christ comes to us and through the Holy Spirit that we are joined to Christ and each other as the Mystical Body of Christ.

By this we can see that the celebration of the Eucharist does not just unite us to God as individuals who are isolated from one another. Rather, we are united to Christ together with all the other members of the Mystical Body. The celebration of the Eucharist should thus increase our love for one another and remind us of our responsibilities toward one another. Furthermore, as members of the Mystical Body, we have a duty to represent Christ and to bring Christ to the world. We have a responsibility to share the Good News of Christ not only by our words but also by how we live our lives. We also have a responsibility to work against all the forces in our world that oppose the Gospel, including all forms of injustice. The *Catechism of the Catholic Church* teaches us: "The Eucharist commits us to the poor. To receive in truth the Body and Blood of Christ given up for us, we must recognize Christ in the poorest, his brethren" (no. 1397).

15 WHY DO WE CALL THE PRESENCE OF CHRIST IN THE EUCHARIST A "MYSTERY"?

The word "mystery" is commonly used to refer to something that escapes the full comprehension of the human mind. In the Bible, however, the word has a deeper and more specific meaning, for it refers to aspects of God's plan of salvation for humanity, which has already begun but will be completed only with the end of time. In ancient Israel, through the Holy Spirit God revealed to the prophets some of the secrets of what he was going to accomplish for the salvation of his people (cf. Am 3:7; Is 21:28; Dan 2:27-45). Likewise, through the preaching and teaching of Jesus, the mystery of "the Kingdom of God" was being revealed to his disciples (Mk 4:11-12). St. Paul explained that the mysteries of

God may challenge our human understanding or may even seem to be foolishness, but their meaning is revealed to the People of God through Jesus Christ and the Holy Spirit (cf. 1 Cor 1:18-25, 2:6-10; Rom 16:25-27; Rev 10:7).

The Eucharist is a mystery because it participates in the mystery of Jesus Christ and God's plan to save humanity through Christ. We should not be surprised if there are aspects of the Eucharist that are not easy to understand, for God's plan for the world has repeatedly surpassed human expectations and human understanding (cf. Jn 6:60-66). For example, even the disciples did not at first understand that it was necessary for the Messiah to be put to death and then to rise from the dead (cf. Mk 8:31-33, 9:31-32, 10:32-34; Mt 16: 21-23, 17:22-23, 20:17-19; Lk 9:22, 9:43-45, 18:31-34). Furthermore, any time that we are speaking of God we need to keep in mind that our human concepts never entirely grasp God. We must not try to limit God to our understanding, but allow our understanding to be stretched beyond its normal limitations by God's revelation.

CONCLUSION

By his Real Presence in the Eucharist Christ fulfils his promise to be with us "always, until the end of the age" (Mt 28:20). As St. Thomas Aquinas wrote, "It is the law of friendship that friends should live together. . . . Christ has not left us without his bodily presence in this our pilgrimage, but he joins us to himself in this sacrament in the reality of his body and blood" (*Summa Theologiae*, III q. 75, a. 1). With this gift of Christ's presence in our midst, the Church is truly blessed. As Jesus told his disciples, referring to his presence among them, "Amen, I say to you, many prophets and righteous people longed to see what you see but did not see it, and to hear what you hear but did not hear it" (Mt 13:17). In the Eucharist the Church both receives the gift of Jesus Christ and gives grateful thanks to God for such a blessing. This thanksgiving is the only proper response, for through this gift of himself in the celebration of the Eucharist under the appearances of bread and wine Christ gives us the gift of eternal life.

> Amen, amen, I say to you, unless you eat the flesh of the Son of Man and drink his blood, you do not have life within you. Whoever eats my flesh and drinks my blood has eternal life, and I will raise him on the last day. For my flesh is true food, and my blood is true drink. . . . Just as the living Father sent me and I have life because of the Father, so also the one who feeds on me will have life because of me. (Jn 6:53-57)

FOR FURTHER READING

Congregation for the Eastern Churches, *Instruction on Liturgy* (January 1996).

Congregation of Rites, *Eucharisticum Mysterium*, Instruction on the Worship of the Eucharist (May 25, 1967).

Pope John Paul II, *Dominicae Cenae*, Letter to the Bishops of the Church on the Mystery and Worship of the Eucharist (February 24, 1980).

Pope Paul VI, *Mysterium Fidei*, Encyclical on the Holy Eucharist (September 3, 1965).

Pope Pius XII, *Mediator Dei*, Encyclical on the Sacred Liturgy (November 20, 1947).

Second Vatican Council, *Sacrosanctum Concilium*, Constitution on the Sacred Liturgy (December 4, 1963).

Subcommittee on the Third Millennium, National Conference of Catholic Bishops, *A Book of Readings on the Eucharist: A Eucharistic Jubilee* (Washington, D.C.: United States Catholic Conference, 2000).

Theological-Historical Commission for the Great Jubilee of the Year 2000, *The Eucharist, Gift of Divine Life* (New York: The Crossroad Publishing Company, 1999).